YOUR KNOWLEDGE HAS VALUE

- We will publish your bachelor's and
  master's thesis, essays and papers

- Your own eBook and book -
  sold worldwide in all relevant shops

- Earn money with each sale

Upload your text at www.GRIN.com
and publish for free

Joe Majerus

How political factors affected the spread of the early Reformation movement

GRIN Verlag

Bibliografische Information der Deutschen Nationalbibliothek:

Die Deutsche Bibliothek verzeichnet diese Publikation in der Deutschen National-
bibliografie; detaillierte bibliografische Daten sind im Internet über http://dnb.d-
nb.de/ abrufbar.

Imprint:

Copyright © 2011 GRIN Verlag GmbH
Druck und Bindung: Books on Demand GmbH, Norderstedt Germany
ISBN: 978-3-656-28090-3

This book at GRIN:

http://www.grin.com/en/e-book/201254/how-political-factors-affected-the-spread-
of-the-early-reformation-movement

Université du Luxembourg
BCE - Histoire
Semestre d'hiver 2010/2011
Cours: Religion and Power in Early Modern Europe

How political factors affected the spread of the early Reformation movement

Joe Majerus
BCE – Histoire (3)

How political factors affected the spread of the early Reformation movement

In early modern Europe, there were arguably few other events of such far-reaching significance and with ultimately such cataclysmic and lasting consequences than the Reformation movement started by Martin Luther. With all the individual and idiosyncratic forms the different protestant denominations were to assume in the following years, they certainly often stood at the centre of events and developments which were to have profound political, religious and social repercussions upon the overall course of early European history, lasting for many decades while plunging large parts of the continent into a long period of internal unrest and cross-national conflicts[1]. Beyond any doubt the reformation imprinted itself upon the lives and works of people throughout various countries and affected the decision-making of entire states in substantial ways, changing forever the face of not only Europe, but even of the entire world through movements eventually spreading all over the globe[2]. In hindsight it may therefore be all too enticing to assume that there simply hadn't been any other possible scenario than for Protestantism to develop the viral power with which it ultimately was to sweep over societies at the time; and that in fact the mere promise and novel nature of its diverging spiritual teachings and religious views from established Catholic doctrines offered by its various proponents alone had sufficed to gain such permanent and widespread a foothold as it ultimately did. Yet to show that it was as well a variety of additional factors - above all pertaining to the power- and geopolitical realm– that ultimately made possible for such irreversible an establishment and rapid diffusion of the Protestant movement will be the principal aim of this essay.

The focus of the following analysis will, however, chiefly lie upon the socio-political and power-political development of the Holy Roman Empire during those most crucial early years of the Reformation. Such an approach does not only seem conducive given the limited space of this paper; but mainly because the territory of the Holy Roman Empire was after all the point of origin of the first Protestant movement, and also largely because it were in fact the inner disposition and external involvements of the Empire which provided at the time the perhaps most fruitful ground for such a movement to assume so rapidly such viral and extensive a quality as the teachings of Martin Luther ultimately did. Whereas in the initial years the Reformation was aided largely by internal factors - although certainly always in close corollary relation with external events-, its swift diffusion in the decade thereafter was to a not unsubstantial extent only possible due to a series of significant external occurrences and developments. How exactly each of these eventually aided the spread of Protestantism will be elaborated at length on the subsequent pages.

---

1 Kennedy, Paul, Rise and fall of the great Powers, New York 1987, p. 70.
2 MacCulloch, Diarmaid, The Reformation. A History, New York 2004, pp. xxi-xxii (Introduction).

To begin with, Martin Luther's Reformation was originally allowed to assume such a dynamic character only because in its very early stages it was in a certain sense simply not deemed important enough by the Catholic to actually give it much thought[3]. Already in its early beginnings it benefited substantially from the fact that whatever inherent dangers might have lain dormant in Luther's teachings with regard to potentially undermining the authority of the Holy Roman Church, the latter was simply too preoccupied with matters largely pertaining to the immediate secular and political realities of the period so as to divert much of its attention to this seemingly only local annoyance[4]. For the time being Pope Leo X. apparently thought it would do to leave the resolution of this admittedly unpleasant, yet hardly upsetting issue largely in the hands of the Augustin order to which Martin Luther adhered to, while for himself the dealing with various political necessities of the time evidently figured far more urgent and worthwhile for the sake and prosperity of the Holy Roman Church.[5]

Yet from early on the teachings of Martin Luther did not merely remain restricted to the local or purely academic level, much as that might have been his original intention[6]. Very soon they also began to assume a more worldly character, and thus next to serving the purpose of the church's internal reformation, they were in equal measure given an important political significance as well. Still, Martin Luther could hardly have succeeded with his proclamations without the help and support of benevolent secular benefactors, notably by Frederic of Saxony. Yet undoubtedly the assistance and protection provided to him were not solely granted on grounds of general good-will or as a noble means for promulgating his cause[7]; larger and comprehensive political considerations were at issue too and thus ultimately played a significant role as well. In this context it is above all interesting to analyse what factors initially induced Frederic of Saxony, a hitherto devout Catholic[8], to grant his firm and unwavering support for a man who increasingly seemed likely of falling out of grace with the ubiquitously influential and powerful Catholic Church. Even if personal motivations for Frederic's intervention might indeed have figured among his reasons for doing so[9], this in itself hardly seems a cause worthwhile for drawing the potential ill-will of the clergy upon himself. More likely, he was probably also led by deeper political expediencies when he chose to support Luther. To begin with, he may on a very basic level have feared for the prestige and reputation of his university at Wittenberg where Luther taught as professor of theology, therefore compelling him to place a protective hand over

---

3   Wallbank, Tailor, Bailkey, Western Civilization, People and Progress, Volume 1, Illinois 1977, p. 216.
4   Lutz, Reformation und Gegenreformation, München 1997, p. 25.
5   MacCulloch, The Reformation, pp. 124-125.
6   Lutz, Reformation und Gegenreformation, p. 25.
7   Frederic of Saxony was in fact anything but a keen follower of Martin Luther's teachings, which was for one suitably expressed by his large collection of relics. Fuchs, Das Zeitalter der Reformation, p.70.
8   MacCulloch, The Reformation, pp. 116-117.
9   Ostensibly Frederic was rather disgruntled when being denied to marry the daughter of Maxmillian, Margarethe. Hofsommer, Johann, Friederich der Weise und die Reformation, Norderstedt 2008, pp. 23-24.

his servant for the sake of the institution's academic renown[10]. And while a personal sense and duty for justice might also have affected his reasoning[11], the teachings of Martin Luther nevertheless also undoubtedly offered Frederic the unique opportunity of ensuring greater personal, political and economical authority within the Holy Roman Empire.

For one, Luther's harsh criticism of the practices of indulgences certainly wasn't unwelcome to Frederic, since naturally the forestalling of the ever-increasing flow of money from his lands into the treasuries of Rome could only be in his own interests[12]. Moreover, by supporting Luther he would also demonstrate that after all it was still *he* who was the sovereign of Saxony, thereby strengthening his own position as a powerful and influential lord within the Empire[13]. This seems all the more evident when considering his rather strained relationship with the Emperor Maxmillian in the latter's final years[14], so that an interference with the internal matters of his estate would certainly not have been to his likening.

Still, Frederic only had so much power as a Kurfürst was able to exercise at the time; and ultimate authority still lay with the Emperor himself. But why then didn't Maximillian I. pursue Luther in a more vigorous and rigorous manner? Again there were mainly political considerations at work, adding in the event only further to the notion of how the once sacrosanct word of the Holy See seemingly ever more often failed to have a bearing upon the decisions of secular authorities. Since during this time it chanced that on account of Maximillian's advanced age the selection of the next Roman Emperor became an ever more eminent matter, the early Reformation movement ultimately benefited greatly by the fact that in order to gain support for his designated successor and grand-son Charles V. Maxmillian depended upon the votes of the Kürfürsten, yet whose decisions he himself could but influence by making extensive promises and concessions to them[15]. In this process it was once again Frederic of Saxony who was to have an important role, one which would eventually serve the Reformation to a not unsubstantial degree[16]. For not only did he withdraw his own candidature[17], but by assuring to vote for the ascension of Charles V. to the throne he first managed to keep the favour and good-will of Maximillian and then eventually even ensured the then new Emperor's official signature on the „Wahlkapitulation", a document of ultimately significant historical value since it bestowed the imperial estates with greater powers in the Empire's decision-making process[18]. Thus both Maximillian and Charles V., while not wanting to risk the support of Frederic – who then himself

---

10 Fuchs, Walther Peter, Das Zeitalter der Reformation, München 2002, p. 70.
11 Fuchs, Das Zeitalter der Reformation, p. 70.
12 Lutz, Reformation und Gegenreformation, p. 24.
13 Hofsommer, Friederich der Weise, Norderstedt 2008, p. 20.
14 Ludolphy, Ingetraut, Friederich der Weise: Kurfürst von Sachsen; 1463 – 1525, Göttingen 1984, p. 195-204.
15 Fuchs, Das Zeitalter der Reformation, p. 73.
16 MacCulloch, The Reformation, p. 116.
17 Ludolphy, Friederich der Weise, p. 217-218.
18 Ludolphy, Friederich der Weise, pp. 221-222.

arguably had a vital part in curtailing the over-all reach of the Emperor's powers - largely gave priority to political requirements over religious matters, yet in the event unwittingly helped pave the way for a concession which would later prove a substantial hindrance for the Emperor's undisputed authority over the whole of his territory. Likewise, Pope Leo X. inadvertently also contributed to the eventual rise of Luther's movement by seeking the support of Frederic the Wise in order to prevent the election of Charles V. to the Holy Roman Throne[19]. To this end, while primarily acting in the secular interests of the Papal State, Leo. X. had agreed to the dealing of Luther's case on German soil, a decision of not unsubstantial consequences since it spared Luther from having to answer himself in front of the Holy See.[20]

In general, the Reformation also availed itself of the politically fragmented landscape of the Holy Roman Empire, above all from its complex constitutional organisation and regulations which ultimately permitted a greater variety of religious views than in a centralized state[21]. Not only did the issuing of the „Wahlkapitulation" guarantee territorial rights and powers to the States, but despite his central authority the Emperor moreover depended to a certain degree on the decisions of the Imperial Diet, so that throughout the reign of Charles V. the subject of jurisdictional authority remained a constant issue of debate between himself and the estates and thus also became an important driving force of the Reformation movement[22]. While in addition obliged to call it into session every time he needed a supplementary amount of money for his political ventures[23], he therefore repeatedly had to rely upon its cooperation. Naturally, the States' support could usually only be secured on a permanent basis if the Emperor himself refrained from interfering too extensively in their internal matters, so that as result they were left with a rather great amount of territorial autonomy. Ultimately it was also this constellation of mutual dependence between the Emperor and the States which allowed for the Reformation too gain a foothold on the local event, if only because the Emperor wasn't really able to revert to any truly comprehensive, or at lest politically advisable means for containing its diffusion.

Just how significant the political influence of the individual States had in the meantime become was then also exemplified by the events following Luther's excommunication, notably the „Diet of Worms" of 1521. Once more it was Frederic of Saxony's bargaining power with the Emperor which made the latter consent to personally hearing Luther out in front of the Diet[24], even tough the usual step following excommunication would have been the instant

---

19 Cohn, H.J., Did bribes induce the German Electors to choose Charles V. as Emperor in 1519? In: German History, Feb 2001, Vol. 19 Issue 1, p. 13.
20 Especially since the possibility of meeting a quicker conviction of heresy upon pronouncing his views in front of the Pope himself, notably without the benefit of Frederic's protection, appears only all too probable. Fuchs, Das Zeitalter der Reformation, p. 70.
21 Western Civilizations: People and Progress, Volume 1, p. 215.
22 Thornhill, Chris, The Holy Empire and the Law: In: German History, Feb 2006, Vol 24 Issue 1, p. 114.
23 Lutz, Reformation und Gegenreformation, pp. 33-34.
24 MacCulloch, The Reformation, p. 131.

pronouncement of outlawry („Reichsacht") against Luther[25]. That Charles V. eventually agreed to the request only further underlines how political expediencies did by now largely outweigh religious considerations, for ultimately even the firm indignation and disapproval of the Pope did not succeed in compelling Charles V. from changing his mind[26].

As it is well known Luther did in the event refuse to recant, much to the chagrin of Charles V. and certainly of the Holy See as well. Primarily on account of the highly consequential fact that it was only *after* Martin Luther had been allowed to promulgate his teachings freely when first the Catholic Church, then Charles V. finally assumed a more vigorous and staunch opposition against him, they now lacked effective and adequate means to fully repress the ever-increasing momentum of his movement. Just as wider political expediencies had prohibited them from taking the matter seriously in its early stages, it was in fact only upon realising that the entire issue might eventually come to have dire ramifications on their political powers as well that they eventually sought to crush it with greater vehemence. Naturally the Papacy viewed Luther's critic with regard to its own purpose and organisation as a threat to its secular foundation and wealth[27], whereas Charles V. perceived the Reformation primarily as an obstacle to the establishment of a Universal European monarchy under his personal reign[28].

For the cause of the Reformation it was, however, overly propitious that despite the threat it posed to both the Holy See and Charles V., the latter two weren't able to coordinate their efforts in order to accomplish this one common goal. Once again it were primarily political factors responsible for this constellation, for despite the Holy Catholic Church's claim to being the sole legitimate representative of God on Earth, even such devout followers such as Charles V. himself ultimately gave greater importance to the power-political necessities of the secular than the spiritual world[29]. With regard to the exclusively worldly realm, the Holy See was in fact rather perceived as a rival than a close ally, of which Charles failure to heed the words of the Pope and above all the open clash between the Empire and the Papal State over territorial disputes in later years - highlighted by the sack of Rome by Imperial troops in 1527 and the temporal imprisonment of the Pope - provide ample testimony.[30]

Since the Holy See had thus failed to exercise its will upon the Emperor for a persecution of Martin Luther prior to the diet of Worms; and also largely because Charles himself honoured his

---

25 Fuchs, Das Zeitalter der Reformation, p. 89.

25 Mai, Klaus-Rüdiger, Der Vatikan. Geschichte einer Weltmacht im Zwielicht, Köln 2010, p.358-361.

27 Above all his *To The Christian Nobility of the German Nation* must have deeply unsettled the Holy See, given that in it Luther openly attacked its claimed spiritual leadership through priesthood and thus by implication the status and authority of the Pope as well.
Rogers, Mark: A dangerous idea? Martin Luther, E.Y. Mullins, and the Priesthood of all Believers. In: Westminster Theological Journal; Spring2010, Vol. 72 Issue 1, pp. 120-123.

28 Fuchs, Das Zeitalter der Reformation, p. 88.

29 Fuchs, Das Zeitalter der Reformation, p. 87.

30 Lutz, Reformation und Gegenreformation, pp. 31-33.

promise to Frederic of Saxony for a save conduct of Luther before the „Reichsacht" pronounced against him would officially come into effect[31], Luther had ultimately been permitted to get away. Thus for mostly political considerations the chance to take out the most prominent and influential figure of the early Reformation movement had not been seized, so that as a result Luther was able to further work out his theses and begin his translation of the Bible. By means of mechanical book reproduction ever more people were thereafter allowed to read for themselves both the word of God as well as Luther's arguments, which ultimately contributed decisively to the spread of the Reformation among the population[32]. And yet although a total repression of the movement had at that point already become an all but impossible eventuality[33], rapid action to that effect might perhaps still have managed to contain at least partially some of its ever-increasing momentum. But again political involvements, although of external nature now, significantly favoured the cause of Protestantism.

Already in its early days the Reformation was aided to a certain degree by the fact that Charles V. spent most of his time outside of the German parts of the Holy Roman Empire in his Spanish residence. This is all the more true for the 1520s, a time of vast political upheavals on the whole of the European continent, when highly pressing and significant events unfolding all about the Empire demanded his perpetual and undivided attention. Thus despite clearly being conscious of the dangers the Reformation movement posed to his aspirations of a Universal monarchy, the more urgent and immediate character of the political necessities he presently faced forced him to first dedicate most of his efforts and time to the latter's successful resolution, thereby rendering impossible a comprehensive repression of the religious movement within the Empire[34]. For years at a time Charles V. was almost constantly involved in a consecutive number of military campaigns and political endeavours in Italy and southern France, seeking to either secure recent strategic gains or to further extent influence upon his neighbours[35]. This, however, largely left his German territories without a strong and decisive leadership, for in the wake of his absence internal matters were largely conveyed to the „Reichsregiment". Yet alone the fact of its organisational disposition – a panel formed by representatives of the Imperial Estates with increasingly diverging interests– made it an all but impossible task to effectively smother protestant tendencies, all the more so because some of its members did already sympathize with Luther's ideas[36].

---

31 MacCulloch, The Reformation, p. 132.
32 Lemieux, Simon, „The Medium and the Message". In: History Review, Dec 2009, Issue 65, p. 28-33.
33 After all other prominent figures, such as Zwingli in Switzerland, had at that time already emerged in order to speak out in public. MacCulloch, The Reformation, p. 136-144.
34 Kennedy, Rise and fall of the great Powers, p. 75.
35 Espinosa, Aurelio, The Grand Strategy of Charles V (1500-1558): Castile, War and Dynastic Property in the Mediterranean. In: Journal of Early Modern History, 2005, Vol. 9 Issue 3/4, pp. 257-258.
36 Fuchs, Das Zeitalter der Reformation, p. 97-100.

The perennial engagement of Charles V. in European affairs was, moreover, to have further repercussions upon social events in the Empire itself, albeit this time in a more subtle manner. Much has been written of the role of the peasants' rebellion in the wider context of the Reformation, yet within the context of this article it is particularly noteworthy that it were not alone internal social causes which eventually led to its over-regional manifestation, but that developments of external nature were indirectly at work as well. For the fact remains that although the movement was eventually crushed, an even earlier, better coordinated and more rigorously conducted repression of the individual rebellion hotspots was insofar hindered by the commitment of the bulk of the Imperial troops in northern Italy (Pavia)[37], so that as a result of this initial lack of firm opposition the rebellion was eventually only allowed to carry its momentum to the territorial level[38]. However, the subsequent episode of vast social upheavals and riots on German lands was, despite Luther's rebuke, to benefit his cause over the long run as well, since in order to prevent any further uprisings many worldly leaders eventually opened themselves up to certain religious reforms[39]. Thus originally aided by external expediencies, the peasants' rebellion substantially affected the reasoning of many princes who, again primarily for political considerations of stability and order, ultimately accepted the Reformation in order to circumvent future public unrest. For if breaking with the church was what it took to avert chaos and anarchy on their territories, than apparently that was something many princes were willing to accept.[40]

Finally, the unbound western expansion of the Ottoman Empire also posed an ever increasing threat to the Empire's eastern borders, so that here too Charles V. was obliged to deal first with this security-political reality before he could possibly divert his attention to the socio-religious developments presently unfolding within his own proper territory[41]. As with regard to the Ottoman Empire in particular, one furthermore also has to keep the common mindset of western civilizations of the time in close perspective. For within a general climate of anxiety and uncertainty as well as profound fear of the future, many people certainly perceived the looming presence of the Muslim Empire on the fringes of central Europe as a divine sign of dark and dismal times ahead, thereby possibly making some of them all the more susceptible for the teachings of a new „prophet" promising a different approach to the driving issues and problems of their time[42].

For multiple political reasons the Reformation movement was thus allowed to thrive and

---

37 MacCulloch, Reformation, p. 159.
38 Lutz, Reformation und Gegenreformation, p. 35-36.
39 MacCulloch, The Reformation, pp. 162-165.
40 MacCulloch, The Reformation, p. 162.
41 Espinosa, The Grand Strategy of Charles V., pp. 250-258.
42 MacCulloch, The Reformation, pp. 152-153.

spread at a rapid rate, mainly because it was missing a strong central authority with the capability to take away some of its momentum[43]. And yet although it certainly remains doubtful as to what extent Charles V. might actually still have been able to impose his will upon the Imperial states with regard to religious matters in the first place, the fact that he was tied by largely external factors ultimately deprived him of the perhaps last possibility of working towards at least the partial restriction of a movement which, having priorly benefited from wider internal considerations already, now in the absence of a more resolute political opposition ultimately couldn't be prevented any longer from firmly and irrevocably establishing itself upon large parts of the Empire's territory, and eventually beyond its borders as well.

---

43 Fuchs, Das Zeitalter der Reformation, p. 129.

Bibliography

- Cohn, H.J., Did bribes induce the German Electors to choose Charles V. as Emperor in 1519? In: German History, Feb 2001, Vol. 19 Issue 1, p1-27, 27p.
- Espinosa, Aurelio, The Grand Strategy of Charles V (1500-1558): Castile, War and Dynastic Property in the Mediterranean. In: Journal of Early Modern History, 2005, Vol. 9 Issue 3/4, p239-283, 45p.
- Lemieux, Simon, „The Medium and the Message". In: History Review, Dec 2009, Issue 65, p28-33, 6p.
- Rogers, Mark: A dangerous idea? Martin Luther, E.Y. Mullins, and the Priesthood of all Believers. In: Westminster Theological Journal; Spring 2010, Vol. 72 Issue 1, p119-134, 16p.
- Thornhill, Chris, The Holy Empire and the Law: In: German History, Feb 2006, Vol. 24 Issue 1, p111-117, 7p.

- Fuchs, Walther Peter, Das Zeitalter der Reformation, C.H. Beck: München 1999.
- Hofsommer, Johann, Friedrich der Weise und die Reformation, Norderstedt 2008
- Kennedy, Paul, Rise and fall of the great Powers, Random House: New York 1987.
- Ludolphy, Ingetraut, Friedrich der Weise: Kurfürst von Sachsen,
- Lutz, Heinrich, Reformation und Gegenreformation, R. Oldenburg Wissenschaftsverlag: München 2002.
- MacCulloch, Diarmaid, The Reformation. A History, Viking Penguin: New York 2004.
- Mai, Klaus-Rüdiger, Der Vatikan. Geschichte einer Weltmacht im Zwielicht, Bastei-Lübbe Verlag: Köln 2010.
- Wallbank, Tailor, Bailkey, Western Civilization: People and Progress, Vol. 1, Scots, Foresman and Company, Illinois 1977.